V&A Pattern
Heal's

V&A Publishing

V&A Pattern
Heal's

First published by V&A Publishing, 2012
V&A Publishing
Victoria and Albert Museum
South Kensington
London SW7 2RL

ISBN 978 1 85177 680 1
Library of Congress Control Number 2011935155

10 9 8 7 6 5 4 3 2 1
2016 2015 2014 2013 2012

A catalogue record for this book is available
from the British Library.

Series Art Direction: Rose
Design: V&A Design

Front cover (A):
Humphrey Spender/Heal's
Sirocco, furnishing fabric. Screen-printed cotton. UK, 1978 (V&A: Circ.211–1954)
Pages 2–3 (B):
Anthony Summers/Heal's
Itaglio, furnishing fabric. Screen-printed cotton. UK, 1973 (V&A: T.492:3–1999)
Page 6 (C):
Lucienne Day/Heal's
Calyx, furnishing fabric. Screen-printed cotton. UK, 1951 (V&A: T.161–1995)
Page 11 (D):
Barbara Brown/Heal's
Galleria, furnishing fabric. Screen-printed cotton satin. UK, 1969 (V&A: Circ.35–1969)
Pages 78–9 (E):
Natalie Gibson/Heal's
Nectar, furnishing fabric. Screen-printed cotton. UK, 1977 (V&A: T.35–1978)

Letters (in brackets) refer to the file name of the
images on the accompanying disc.

Printed in China

V&A Publishing

Supporting the world's leading
museum of art and design,
the Victoria and Albert
Museum, London

V&A Pattern

Each *V&A Pattern* book is an introduction to the Victoria and Albert Museum's extraordinarily diverse collection. The museum has more than three million designs for textiles, decorations, wallpapers and prints; some well-known, others less so. This series explores pattern-making in all its forms, across the world and through the centuries. The books are intended to be both beautiful and useful – showing patterns to enjoy in their own right and as inspiration for new design.

V&A Pattern presents the greatest names and styles in design, while also highlighting the work of anonymous draughtsmen and designers, often working unacknowledged in workshops, studios and factories, and responsible for designs of aesthetic originality and technical virtuosity. Many of the most interesting and imaginative designs are seen too rarely. *V&A Pattern* gathers details from our best objects and hidden treasures from pattern books, swatch books, company archives, design records and catalogues to form a fascinating introduction to the variety and beauty of pattern at the V&A.

The compact disc at the back of each book invites you to appreciate the ingenuity of the designs, and the endless possibilities for their application. To use the images professionally, you need permission from V&A Images, as the V&A controls – on behalf of others – the rights held in its books and CD-Roms. *V&A Pattern* can only ever be a tiny selection of the designs available at www.vandaimages.com. We see requests to use images as an opportunity to help us to develop and improve our licensing programme – and for us to let you know about images you may not have found elsewhere.

Heal's
Mary Schoeser

In 1946, Heal's Wholesale and Export Limited commissioned
a range of furnishing fabrics for the first time. The wholesale
branch of the family firm – established in London by John
Harris Heal in 1810 – had begun in 1941 in order to export
a range of goods made from war surplus stock, and added
textiles to their range in 1944. But, created under the direction
of Prudence Maufe and Tom Worthington, the launch of the
1946 new ranges had two other interrelated functions aside
from the essential post-war need to export: to boost the
stock for the store's retail fabric department (which before
the Second World War had offered continental and British
textiles, including some designed by Christopher Heal); and to
complement their modern furniture, much of which was still
made in Heal's own workshops.

In 1946 cotton cloth was still in restricted supply, so their
patterns were screen-printed on to linen. The designs reflected
other post-war requirements, being small in repeat size
in order to minimize wastage, and with colours limited to
three or four. The results were nonetheless striking, and the
limited number of colours in any one design was to become
a hallmark of many subsequent Heal's textiles. However, by
1950 the success of the ranges encouraged the firm to begin
roller-printing some designs. This technique required the sale
of much more cloth to be profitable, but reduced the price to
the consumer, as did printing on cotton as opposed to linen,

also begun in 1950. With some of their fabrics now affordable for far more people, the influence of Heal's textiles grew. They garnered international attention when Lucienne Day's 'Calyx' (p.6) won a gold medal at the Milan Triennale in 1951, followed by the American Institute of Decorators' prize awarded in 1952. Over the following two decades Day contributed over 70 designs to the ranges and Heal's – with designs by Day and others – won many more awards.

Day was not the only designer to help establish Heal's reputation for avant-garde furnishing textiles. During their first ten years commissioning textiles, Heal's produced designs by over 75 designers, many of whom contributed several designs a year for a number of years. Most prominent among these were Helen Close, Jane Edgar and Dorothy Martin. Many designs were bought from recent graduates of London's Central School of Art and Design and Royal College of Art. Established designers were also sought out; among these in the 1950s were Harold Cohen, Hilda Dirkin, Roger Nicholson, Paule Vézelay and Willy Hermann, the latter with an influential design studio in Germany.

By 1959, having changed their name to Heal Fabrics Ltd and advertising themselves simply as Heal's, they were exporting to over 25 world markets. In Germany the company was so successful that by September 1964 they had established a wholly owned subsidiary in Stuttgart: Heal Textil GmbH. Now large-scale designs by Barbara Brown, Doreen Dyall and Peter Hall were most frequently found in their ranges but, as before, many others contributed. With the company issuing around 30 designs each year, there were, for example, 24 designers represented in the 1965 range, 16 in the 1969 range and 17 in 1974, including some sourced through their Stuttgart branch. Tom Worthington was responsible for selecting all designs as Managing Director from 1948 until 1971, and he and his assistant Jenni Allan (who did the colourways) saw some 12,000 designs annually, buying around 80 each year.

The ranges reflected Worthington's interest in parallel trends in the fine arts, and he was known to produce 'uncommercial' designs, remarking in *Design* (vol.269, 1971) that 'It may take a year or longer for a really advanced design to start selling... And sometimes an avant-garde design – although not selling itself – can gain so much publicity it will create a market for similar designs'. To further these intentions, Heal's fabrics were issued with a brief biography of the designer, including lists of their prizes or awards. Worthington promoted young designers particularly. This was so much the case that Evelyn Redgrave, who started designing for Heal's in 1969 while still a student at Hornsey College of Art, London, became a Design Director by 1974.

A second Heal's store was opened in Guildford in 1972, but expansion was soon halted by the oil crisis, which plunged the country, and Heal's, into difficult times. Although the fabric division continued to produce striking designs and attract favourable press commentary, attempts to further bring down prices and broaden their appeal to include furnishings for children's rooms, were unsuccessful. Neil Bradburn's popular 1974 pattern 'Small Elephants' (pl.63), for example, was reissued in 1976 on a much larger scale as 'Elephants', and printed on a cheaper cotton cloth. The manufacturing records, which are held in the V&A's Archive of Art and Design, indicate initial production of about 820 metres, and no more. Redgrave, having completed work on the 1977 range (which included designs by Collier Campbell, Natalie Gibson and Humphrey Spender, among others), left to set up her own textile company, Tarian, which took on some of the Heal's production. Oliver Heal, on becoming Managing Director in 1980, tried, as the store's history tells it, 'to stem the losses and claw back Heal's reputation' (*A History of Heal's*, 1984), but in 1983 the family firm was sold to Terence Conran under the Storehouse group umbrella.

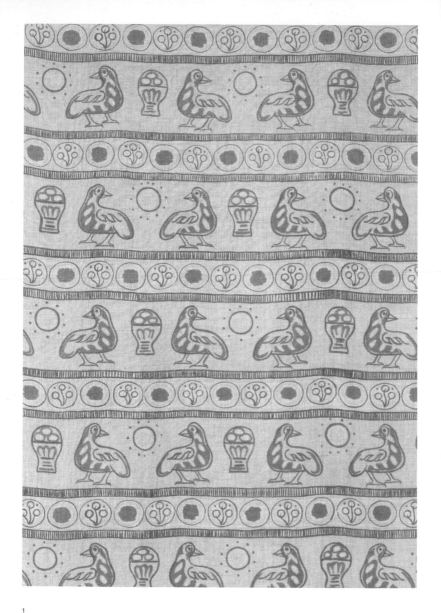

1
Jane Edgar/Heal's
Hedgerow, furnishing fabric. Screen-printed linen. UK, 1947 (V&A: Circ.344–1948)

2
Jane Edgar/Heal's
Mexican Market, furnishing fabric. Screen-printed linen. UK, 1947 (V&A: Circ.215–1948)

3
Dorothy Lipton/Heal's
Sunflower, furnishing fabric. Screen-printed linen. UK, 1948 (V&A: Circ.341–1948)

4
Jane Edgar/Heal's
Coq Rouane, furnishing fabric. Screen-printed linen. UK, c.1950 (V&A: Circ.360–1999)

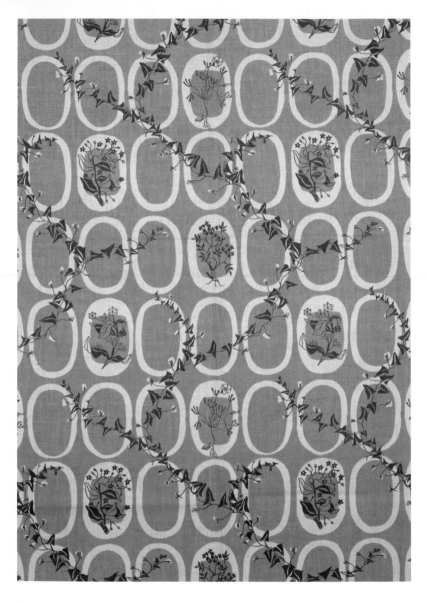

5
Lucienne Day/Heal's
Fluelin, furnishing fabric. Roller-printed cotton. UK, 1950 (V&A: Circ.205–1951)

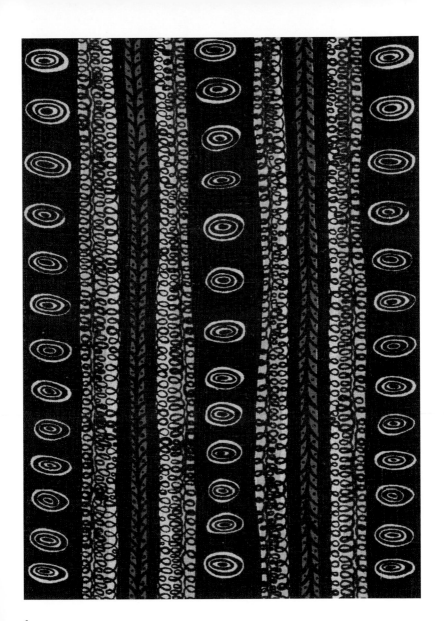

6
Dorothy Hall/Heal's
Target, furnishing fabric. Roller-printed cotton. UK, 1950 (V&A: T.395:5–1999)

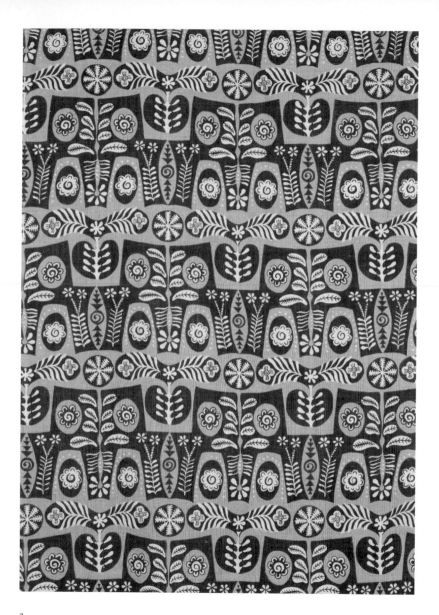

7
Roger Nicholson/Heal's
Lacy, furnishing fabric. Screen-printed linen. UK, 1951 (V&A: Circ.207–1951)

8
Jane Edgar/Heal's
Courtyard, furnishing fabric. Screen-printed linen. UK, 1952 (V&A: T.362–1999)

9
Roger Nicholson/Heal's
Matura, furnishing fabric. Roller-printed cotton. UK, 1951 (V&A: Circ.206–1951)

10
Lucienne Day/Heal's
Flotilla, furnishing fabric. Screen-printed rayon. UK, 1952 (V&A: Circ.51–1953)

11
Sylvia Chambers/Heal's
Jaborandi, furnishing fabric. Screen-printed linen. UK, 1953 (V&A: Circ.55–1953)

12
Hilda Durkin/Heal's
Village Church, furnishing fabric. Screen-printed cotton. UK, 1954 (V&A: Circ.212–1954)

13
Lucienne Day/Heal's
Graphica, furnishing fabric. Screen-printed cotton. UK, 1954 (V&A: Circ.211–1954)

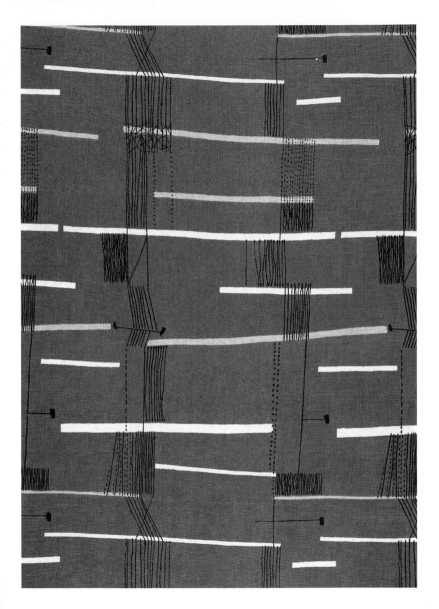

14
Lucienne Day/Heal's
Springboard, furnishing fabric. Screen-printed linen. UK, 1954 (V&A: Circ.209–1954)

15
Mary White/Heal's
Coppice, furnishing fabric (see also plate 16). Screen-printed cotton. UK, 1954 (V&A: T.545:1–1999)

16
Mary White/Heal's
Coppice, furnishing fabric (see also plate 15). Screen-printed cotton. UK, 1954 (T.545:4–1999)

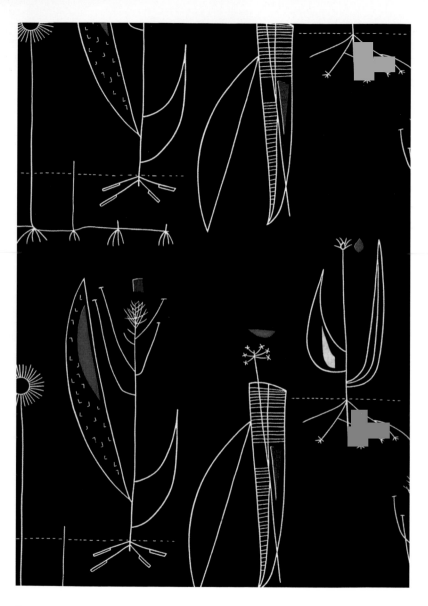

17
Lucienne Day/Heal's
Herb Anthony, furnishing fabric. Screen-printed cotton. UK, 1955 (V&A: Circ.482–1956)

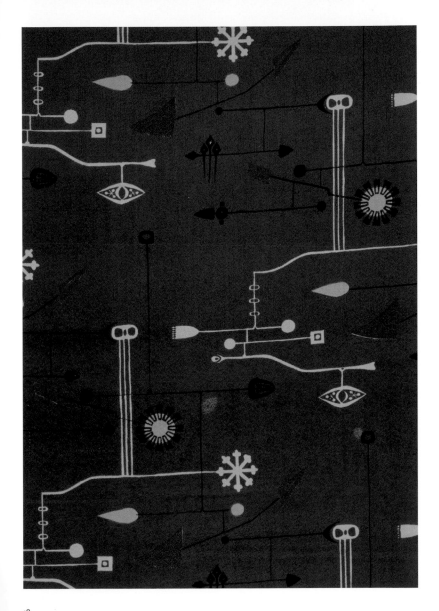

18
June Lyon/Heal's
Mobile, furnishing fabric. Screen-printed rayon satin. UK, 1954 (V&A: Circ.208–1954)

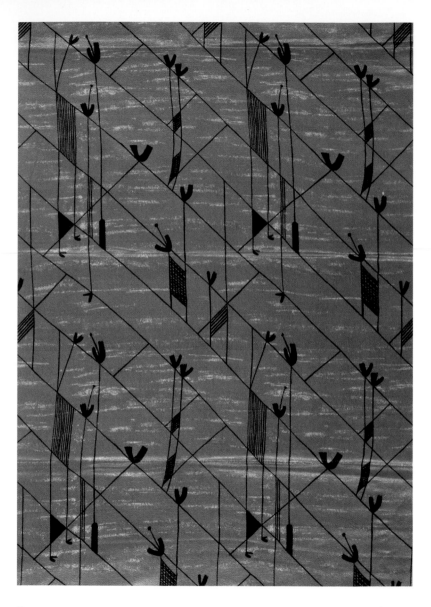

19
Lucienne Day/Heal's
Chequers, furnishing fabric. Screen-printed cotton satin. UK, 1954 (V&A: Circ.207–1954)

20
Michael O'Connell/Heal's
Syncromesh, furnishing fabric. Screen-printed cotton. UK, 1957 (V&A: Circ.65A–1957)

21
Heal's
Berkley, furnishing fabric. Woven wool-faced moquette. UK, 1956 (V&A: Circ.487B–1956)

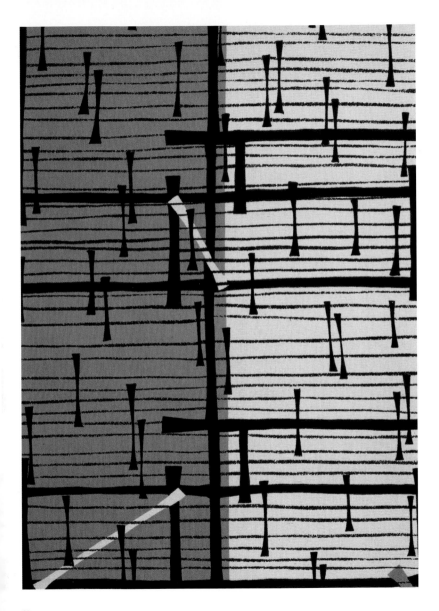

22
Françoise Lelong/Heal's
Projection, furnishing fabric. Screen-printed cotton. UK, 1956 (V&A: Circ.484–1956)

23
Mary Moran/Heal's
Daffodil, furnishing fabric. Screen-printed bark cloth. UK, 1957 (V&A: Circ.69B–1957)

24
Paule Vézelay/Heal's
Variations, furnishing fabric. Screen-printed cotton. UK, 1957 (V&A:T.284–2000)

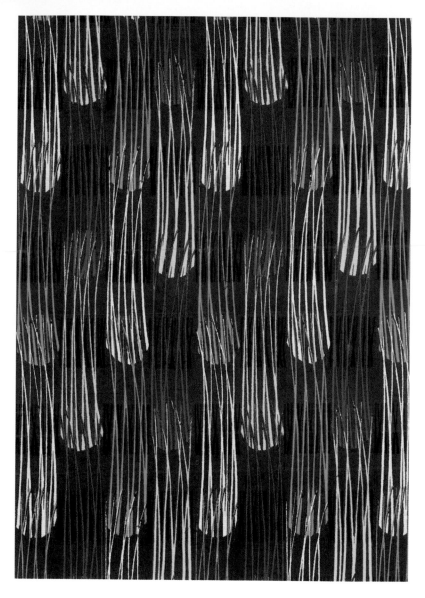

25
Willy Hermann/Heal's
Reeden, furnishing fabric. Roller-printed cotton. UK, 1957 (V&A: Circ.67–1957)

26
Dorothy Carr/Heal's
Oak, furnishing fabric. Screen-printed cotton satin. UK, 1958 (V&A: Circ.45–1958)

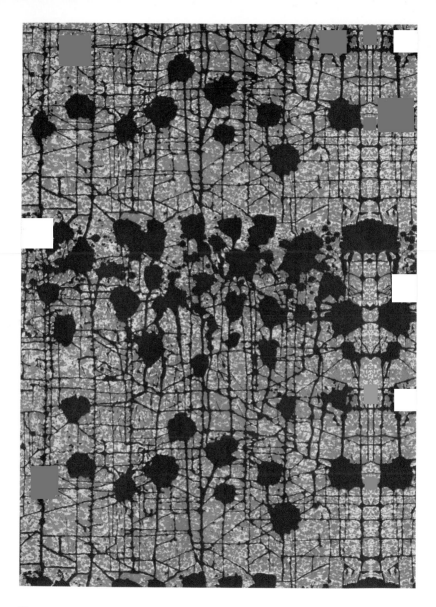

27
Harold Cohen/Heal's
Vineyard, furnishing fabric. Screen-printed cotton. UK, 1959 (V&A: Circ.38–1959)

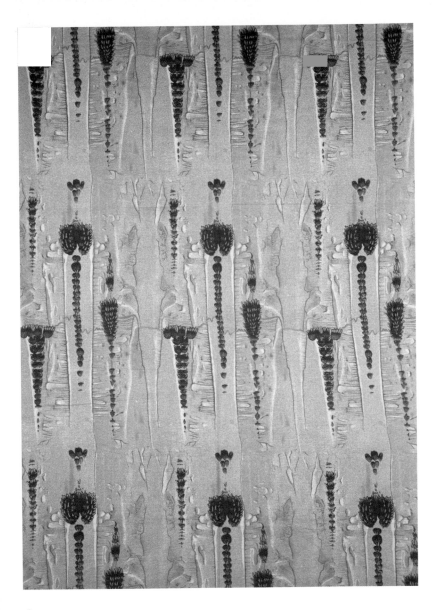

28
Gordon Dent/Heal's
Thistle, furnishing fabric. Screen-printed cotton. UK, 1961 (V&A: T.338:2–1999)

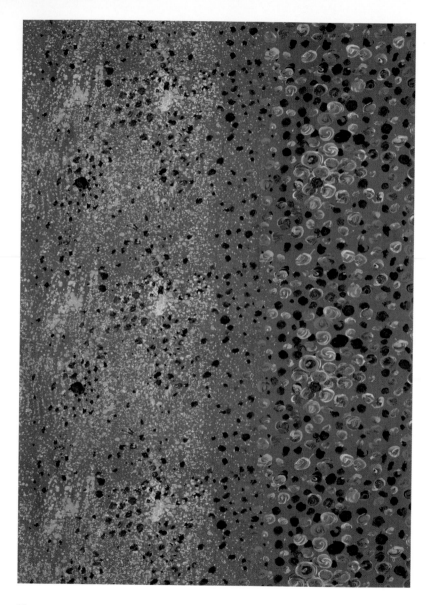

29
Doreen Dyall/Heal's
Pebbles, furnishing fabric. Screen-printed cotton. UK, 1960 (V&A:Circ.258–1960)

30
Howard Carter/Heal's
Sunflower, furnishing fabric. Screen-printed crêpe-weave cotton. UK, 1962 (V&A: Circ.598–1963)

31
Barbara Brown/Heal's
Intermission, furnishing fabric. Screen-printed cotton. UK, 1960 (V&A: Circ.250–1960)

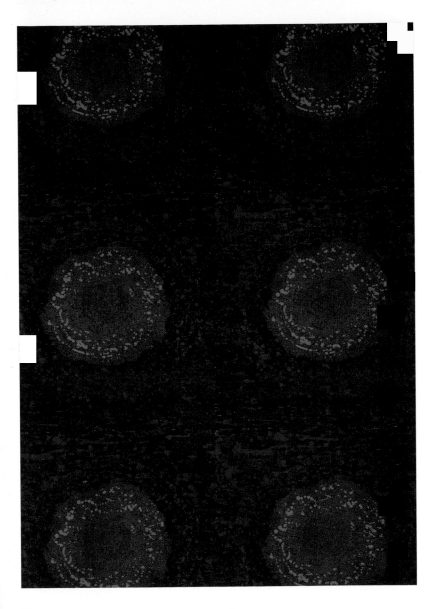

32
Fay Hillier/Heal's
Corona, furnishing fabric. Screen-printed cotton crêpe. UK, 1962 (V&A: Circ.2–1962)

33
Barbara Brown/Heal's
Recurrence, furnishing fabric. Screen-printed cotton crêpe. UK, 1962 (V&A: Circ.657–1962)

34
Barbara Brown/Heal's
Reciprocation, furnishing fabric. Screen-printed cotton. UK, 1962 (V&A: Circ.656–1962)

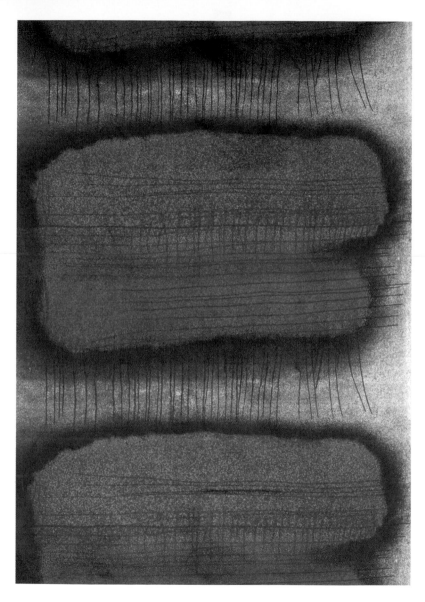

35
Doreen Dyall/Heal's
Serenity, furnishing fabric. Screen-printed cotton satin. UK, 1964 (V&A: Circ.753–1964)

36
Colleen Farr/Heal's
Watermeadow, furnishing fabric. Screen-printed cotton. UK, 1964 (V&A: T.370:6–1999)

37
Barbara Brown/Heal's
Expansion, furnishing fabric. Screen-printed cotton satin. UK, 1966 (V&A: Circ.269–1967)

38
Evelyn Brooks/Heal's
Impact, furnishing fabric. Screen-printed cotton. UK, 1965 (V&A: Circ.250–1967)

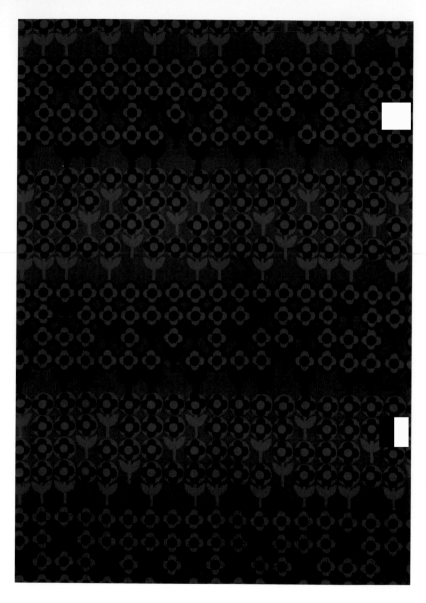

39
Peter Hall/Heal's
Verdure, furnishing fabric. Screen-printed cotton. UK, 1965 (V&A: Circ.257–1967)

40
Doreen Dyall/Heal's
Focus, furnishing fabric. Screen-printed cotton satin. UK, 1965 (V&A: Circ.255–1967)

41
Barbara Brown/Heal's
Decor, furnishing fabric. Screen-printed cotton. UK, 1966 (V&A: Circ.265–1967)

42
Peter Hall/Heal's
Petrus, furnishing fabric. Screen-printed cotton. UK, 1967 (V&A: Circ.28–1968)

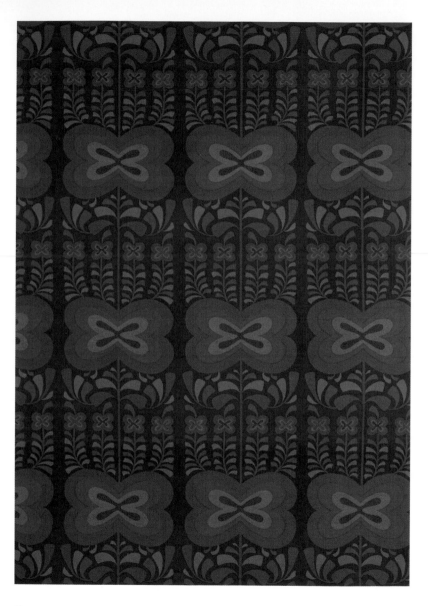

43
Jyoti Bhomik/Heal's
Indian Summer, furnishing fabric. Screen-printed cotton crêpe. UK, 1966 (V&A: Circ.261–1967)

44
Peter Hall/Heal's
Tivoli, furnishing fabric. Screen-printed cotton. UK, 1967 (V&A: Circ.27–1968)

45
Haydon Williams/Heal's
Extension, furnishing fabric. Screen-printed cotton. UK, 1967 (V&A: Circ.30–1968)

46
Barbara Brown/Heal's
Complex, furnishing fabric. Screen-printed cotton. UK, 1967 (V&A: Circ.31–1968)

47
Lucienne Day/Heal's
Sunrise, furnishing fabric. Screen-printed cotton. UK, 1969 (V&A: Circ.39–1969)

48
Janet Taylor/Heal's
Arcade, furnishing fabric. Screen-printed cotton. UK, 1969 (V&A: Circ.30–1969)

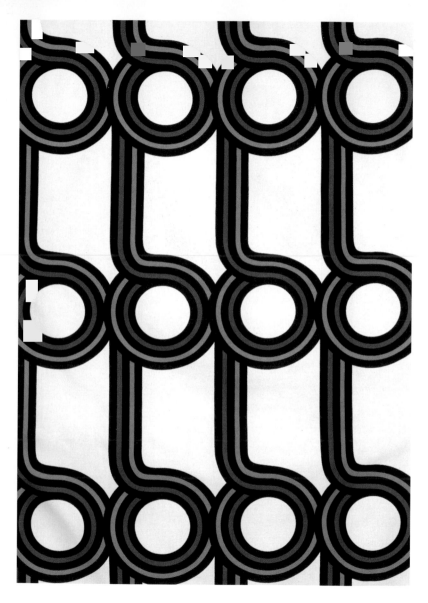

49
Anne Fehlow/Heal's
Perimeter, furnishing fabric. Screen-printed cotton. UK, 1969 (V&A: Circ.782–1969)

50
Peter Hall/Heal's
Volution, furnishing fabric. Screen-printed cotton satin. UK, 1969 (V&A: Circ.40–1969)

51
Hamdi El Atlar/Heal's
Lariat, furnishing fabric. Screen-printed cotton. UK, 1969 (V&A: Circ.36–1969)

52
Barbara Brown/Heal's
Spiral, furnishing fabric. Screen-printed cotton satin. UK, 1969 (V&A: Circ.784–1969)

53
Barbara Brown/Heal's
Ikebana, furnishing fabric. Screen-printed cotton satin. UK, 1970 (V&A: Circ.141–1976)

54
Barbara Brown/Heal's
Gyration, furnishing fabric. Screen-printed cotton satin. UK, 1971 (V&A: Circ.140–1976)

55
Heather Brown/Heal's
Furnishing fabric. Screen-printed cotton. UK, 1972 (V&A: Circ.7–1972)

56
David Bartle/Heal's
Fandango, furnishing fabric. Screen-printed cotton satin. UK, 1973 (V&A: T.253:2–1999)

57
Juliusz Heller/Heal's
Splash, furnishing fabric. Screen-printed cotton. UK, 1973 (V&A: T.404–1999)

58
Peter Hall/Heal's
Rosamund, furnishing fabric. Screen-printed cotton. UK, 1975 (V&A: T.392:1–1999)

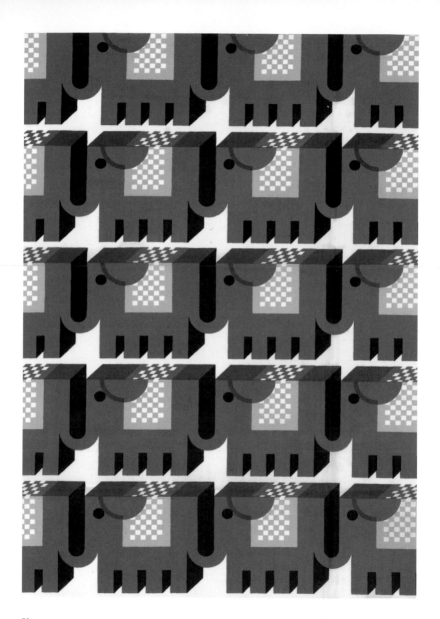

59
Neil Bradburn/Heal's
Small Elephants, furnishing fabric. Printed cotton. UK, 1974 (V&A: T.268:3–1999)

60
Humphrey Spender/Heal's
Sirocco, furnishing fabric. Printed cotton. UK, 1978 (V&A: Circ.211–1954)

61
Mary Oliver/Heal's
Lily Pond, furnishing fabric. Screen-printed cotton. UK, 1976 (V&A: Circ.2–1976)

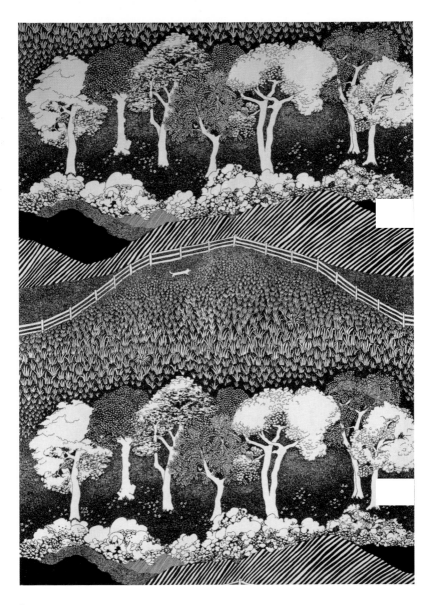

62
Jennie Foley/Heal's
Country Walk, furnishing fabric. Screen-printed cotton satin. UK, 1976 (V&A: Circ.1–1976)

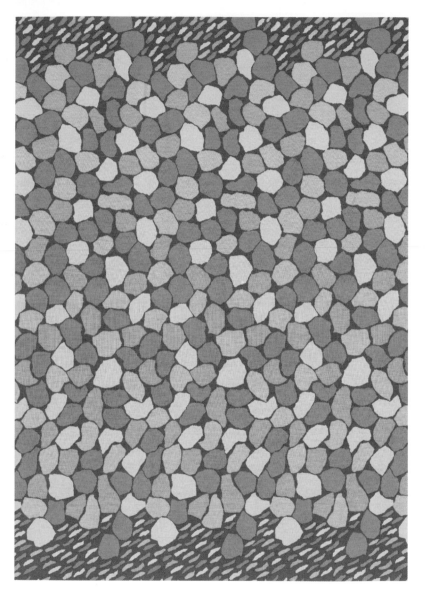

63
Annabel Ralphs/Heal's
Maze, furnishing fabric. Screen-printed cotton. UK, 1978 (T.474:2–1999)

64
Collier Campbell/Heal's
Side Show, furnishing fabric. Screen-printed cotton. UK, 1977 (T.36–1978)

James Morgan/Heal's
Rose, furnishing fabric. Screen-printed cotton satin. UK, 1974 (V&A: Circ.184–1974)

66
Hansjurgen Holzer/Heal's
Square Dance, furnishing fabric. Screen-printed cotton satin. UK, 1980 (V&A: T.415:2–1999)

Further Reading

Breward, Christopher
and Wilcox, Clare, ed.
The Ambassador Magazine
London, 2012

Jackson, Lesley
*20th-Century
Pattern Design*
New York, 2007

Parry, Linda et al.
British Textiles
London, 2010

Prichard, Sue
V&A Pattern: The Fifties
London, 2009

Digital Images

The patterns reproduced in this book are stored on the accompanying compact disc as jpeg files (at approximately A5-size, 300 dpi). You should be able to open them, and manipulate them, direct from the CD-ROM in most modern image software (on Windows or Mac platforms), and no installation should be required (although we, as publishers, cannot guarantee absolutely that the disk will be accessible for every computer).

Instructions for tracing and tiling the images will be found with the documentation for your software.

The names of the files correspond to the V&A inventory numbers of the images.

Copyright

All of the images are © Victoria and Albert Museum, London, and you may not pass them on to a third party.

These images are for your personal use and enjoyment only. Any commercial applications (by which we mean work intended to generate any form of revenue) must be approved by V&A Images via www.vandaimages.com

Our commitment to inspiring design means that securing permissions should be both reasonable and quick. We believe in fair use, but in no event shall VAE (Victoria and Albert Enterprises Ltd) be liable for any damages whatsoever (including but not limited to damages for loss of profit or loss of data) related to the use, or inability to use, this resource.

We want you to use the images, but please respect our intellectual property.